15 Minute Paleo

Quick & Easy Gluten-Free Recipes and Paleo Dinners in 15 Minutes or Less

Lucy Fast

Lucy Fast

Just to say Thank You for Purchasing this Book I want to give you a gift 100% absolutely FREE

A Copy of My Upcoming Special Report "*Paleo Pantry: The Beginner's Guide to What Should and Should NOT be in Your Paleo Kitchen*"

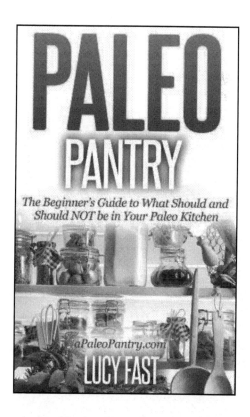

Go to www.aPaleoPantry.com to Reserve Your FREE Copy

Table of Contents

Introduction

I want to thank you and congratulate you for purchasing the book, "15 Minute Paleo: Quick & Easy Gluten-Free Recipes and Paleo Dinners in 15 Minutes or Less". This book contains proven steps and strategies on how to cook delicious, easy, and healthy meals in 15 minutes or less. If you are a busy Mom or Dad, and tend to grab take-out for your family a little too often, then this book was created just for you! With this book in hand, you can learn the ins and outs of creating healthy meals for your family in just 15 minutes. We've include delicious red meat, poultry, fish and soup recipes that can all be created in your kitchen with very few ingredients and very little time. With this book, you can learn the secrets of quick Paleo cooking and can stop feeling guilty every time you bring home take-out.

Thanks again for purchasing this book, I hope you enjoy it!

Meat Mains in Minutes

Beef Strip Salad

Servings: 4
Prep Time: 10 minutes
Cook Time: 15 minutes

Ingredients:
1 head lettuce
1 bunch spinach
1 tomato
1 cup baby carrots
4 radishes
½ cup frozen green peas
½ cup frozen corn
½ head broccoli
½ head cauliflower
10 strips beef flank steak strips

Directions:
1. Season beef with salt and pepper, then cook over medium heat to the degree of doneness you prefer (flank steak is usually more tasty in the mid-rare range – it's not too chewy, and not too tough)
2. While the beef is cooking, chop up the lettuce and add it to a large bowl.
3. Throw the spinach leaves into the bowl.
4. Dice the tomato, baby carrots, radishes, broccoli and cauliflower and add them to the salad.
5. Place ½ cup of frozen corn and ½ cup of frozen peas in a microwave safe bowl and heat the veggies up in the microwave in 30 second intervals until they are defrosted. Add the defrosted veggies to your salad.

6. Once the beef is finished, throw it on top of your salad.
7. Serve.

Stuffed Peppers

Servings: 4
Prep Time: 5 minutes
Cook Time: 10 minutes

Ingredients:
2 Red Bell Peppers
8 strips of Bacon
4 Eggs
1 Bunch Spinach
Salt and Pepper to Taste

Directions:
1. Preheat your oven to 425°F.
2. Cut the tops off of the red peppers and remove their seeds. Next, cut the peppers lengthwise and lay them on a foil-lined baking sheet.
3. Tear the spinach into small pieces and fill each pepper half with spinach.
4. Next, crack an egg into each pepper half, and sprinkle with salt and pepper.
5. Bake for 10 minutes, or until the eggs have fully cooked.
6. While the peppers are cooking, fry 10 strips of bacon over medium heat in a skillet.
7. After removing the peppers from the oven, chop up the bacon and sprinkle it over each pepper.

Cube Steaks with Mushrooms

Servings: 4
Prep Time: 2-3 minutes
Cook Time: 12 minutes

Ingredients:
4 cube steaks, defrosted
1 cup beef broth
3 cloves garlic, minced
1 teaspoon dried thyme
1 white onion, diced
2 cups button mushrooms, diced
Salt and pepper to taste

Directions:
1. Lay the defrosted cube steaks in a large skillet and sprinkle with salt and pepper.
2. Turn your stove on medium-high temperature, then pour the beef broth over the cube steaks.
3. Sprinkle the minced garlic, onions, mushrooms and thyme over the meat then cover and cook for 8 minutes.
4. After 8 minutes, flip the meat and stir the mushrooms. Cover and cook for another 4-5 minutes, or until the meat is cooked through.
5. Serve with a tossed Salad.

Scotch Eggs

Servings: 3
Prep Time: 2-3 minutes
Cook Time: 12 minutes

Ingredients:
6 peeled hard boiled eggs
1 lb. lean ground pork sausage
1 teaspoon salt
½ teaspoon pepper

Directions:
1. Preheat your oven to 400° F.
2. Mix the salt, pepper and ground sausage together in a mixing bowl.
3. Carefully scoop out ⅓ cup of pork and form it into a pattie in your hands. Lay one hard-boiled egg into the middle of the patty and encase the egg with meat.
4. Repeat with remaining eggs and sausage.
5. Place the scotch eggs on a foiled lined baking sheet and bake for 12 minutes or until sausage is cooked through.

Hamburgers on Lettuce Buns

Servings: 4
Prep Time: 5 minutes
Cook Time: 10 minutes

Ingredients:
8 leaves lettuce
1 lb. ground beef
1 teaspoon Salt
1 teaspoon pepper
1/2 teaspoon cayenne pepper
½ teaspoon garlic powder
½ teaspoon onion powder

Directions:
1. Mix all of the spices and ground beef together.
2. Divide the ground beef into four equal portions and form each portion into thin patties.
3. Cook the patties in a skillet over medium heat for 5 minutes per side.
4. Serve on two pieces of lettuce with any veggies and Paleo friendly condiments you choose.

Poultry Made Pronto!

Tarragon Chicken

Servings: 4
Prep Time: 5 minutes
Cook Time: 10 minutes

Ingredients:
2 boneless, skinless chicken breasts
1/4 teaspoon salt
1 teaspoon grated lemon rind
1/4 lemon, juiced
2 cloves Garlic, minced
2 teaspoons fresh tarragon

Directions:
1. Cut each chicken breast in half and place the halves in between two pieces of plastic wrap. Pound the chicken to 1/4 inch thickness, then lay them in a non-stick skillet.
2. Sprinkle the chicken breasts with salt, then combine the oil, lemon rind, lemon juice, minced garlic and tarragon in a small bowl. Pour the mixture over the chicken and cook for 2 minutes per side.
3. Next, cover the chicken and simmer on low for about 10 minutes, or until done.
4. Serve with a sautéed vegetable or garden salad for a complete meal.

Chicken with Shiitake Mushrooms

Servings: 4
Prep Time: 5 minutes
Cook Time: 15 minutes

Ingredients:
2 boneless, skinless chicken breasts
1/4 teaspoon salt
¼ teaspoon black pepper
3 cups shiitake mushrooms, sliced (you can substitute with button mushrooms or any other kind you have on hand)
2 green onions, chopped
2 tablespoons clarified butter

Directions:
1. Cut each chicken breast in half and place the halves in between two pieces of plastic wrap. Pound the chicken to ¼ inch thickness, then sprinkle with salt and pepper.
2. Cook the chicken breasts in a non-stick skillet for 4 minutes per each side. Remove the chicken, then add the shiitake mushrooms, green onions and clarified butter to the pan.
3. Cook for about 5 minutes (until mushrooms begin to release their juices), then pour them over the chicken breasts to serve.

Chicken & Veggie Sauté

Servings: 4
Prep Time: 5 minutes
Cook Time: 10 minutes

Ingredients:
1 ½ cups skinless, boneless rotisserie chicken, chopped
½ cup button mushrooms, chopped
¾ teaspoon salt
½ cup zucchini, chopped
½ cup carrot, chopped
3 cloves garlic, minced
1 teaspoon black pepper

Directions:
1. Add everything but the chicken to a sauté pan and cook over medium heat for 5-10 minutes, or until the veggies are tender.
2. While vegetable are cooking, pull the chicken off the bones and chop into bite-size pieces.
3. In the last minute or two of cooking add the chicken and the juices from the rotisseries container to the pan, and heat through.

Walnut Chicken Salad

Servings: 4
Prep Time: 5 minutes
Cook Time: 10 minutes

Ingredients:
2 cups boneless, skinless rotisserie chicken, chopped
1 cup walnuts, chopped
6 cups mixed greens
4 cups spinach
1 chopped hard-boiled egg
½ cup green peas
½ cup tomatoes, diced

Directions:
1. In a salad bowl combine the mixed greens, spinach, egg, green peas, and tomatoes.
2. Add the chopped walnuts and cold chopped chicken.
3. Toss with your dressing of choice and serve.

Quick Mustard Vinaigrette

1 glove of garlic, smashed
2 tablespoons of balsamic vinegar (or any vinegar you like)
1 teaspoon Dijon mustard
5-6 tablespoons oil (any kind other will do)
pinch of dried parsley
pinch of dried thyme
salt and freshly ground pepper to taste

1. In a clean jar or small bowl, add the vinegar, garlic, mustard, parsley and thyme, and mix well.

2. Slowly add the olive oil while either whisking or stirring rapidly with your fork.
3. Add salt and pepper, taste and adjust seasonings.

Herbed Chicken

Servings: 4
Prep Time: 2 minutes
Cook Time: 10 minutes

Ingredients:
2 boneless, skinless chicken breasts
1 tablespoon olive oil
1 shallot, minced
½ cup chicken broth
2 tablespoons fresh parsley
1 tablespoon fresh basil

Directions:
1. Cut your chicken breasts in half, then place the halves in between two pieces of plastic wrap. Pound until they are ¼ inch in thickness.
2. Pour 1 tablespoon of olive oil into a medium skillet, then place the chicken breasts into the skillet. Cook for 3 minutes per side over medium-high heat.
3. After cooking both sides of the chicken breasts, pour the chicken broth into the skillet and add the shallot, fresh parsley and fresh basil.
4. Cover and simmer for 3-4 minutes.

Chicken Burgers with Avocado

Servings: 2
Prep Time: 5 minutes
Cook Time: 10 minutes

Ingredients:
1 lb. ground chicken
1 avocado
1 cup cherry tomatoes
1 red bell pepper
Salt and pepper to Taste

Directions:
1. Divide the ground chicken into 2 equal portions and flatten each portion into a patty. Sprinkle the patties with salt and pepper.
2. Heat a medium skillet over medium-high heat, then cook each burger for 4 minutes on each side.
3. Mash the avocado together with salt and pepper. Add chopped tomatoes and red bell pepper to the avocado and mix.
4. Serve the burgers with the avocado mix on top.

Fast Fish and Speedy Seafood

Shrimp Stir Fry

Servings: 4
Prep Time: 5 minutes
Cook Time: 10 minutes

Ingredients:
20 peeled-deveined shrimp, tails removed
1 red bell pepper, chopped
1 yellow bell pepper, chopped
1 cup snow peas
1 cup baby corn, diced
1 cup button mushrooms, chopped
3 cloves garlic, minced
1 tablespoon olive oil
Salt and pepper to Taste

Directions:
1. Sauté the shrimp and garlic in 1 tablespoon of oil until shrimp is pink and cooked through.
2. Add the veggies and mushrooms to the pan and cook for 5 minutes, stirring frequently.
3. Add salt and pepper to taste and stir to combine.

Bacon Wrapped Smoked Salmon Peppers

Servings: 4
Prep Time: 2 minutes
Cook Time: 15 minutes

Ingredients:
5 strips of bacon (thin bacon works better than thick cut for this recipe)
10 mini sweet peppers, any color
5 ounces smoked salmon

Directions:
1. Preheat your oven to 400°F.
2. Cut each bacon strip in half lengthwise.
3. Cut the tops off of each sweet pepper and remove the seeds.
4. Stuff the peppers with smoked salmon, then wrap the peppers with bacon.
5. Lay the peppers on a foil lined baking sheet and bake for 10-15 minutes, or until the bacon is crispy.

Tuna Tapenade

Servings: 4
Prep Time: 5 minutes
Cook Time: 10 minutes

Ingredients:
¼ cup Kalamata olives, chopped
¼ cup red bell peppers, chopped
2 tablespoons capers (any type will do, but if you can find the ones packed in salt, rather than brine, they taste the best)
2 tablespoons fresh basil
4 Ahi tuna fillets
2 tablespoons olive oil
Salt and pepper to taste
Lemon

Directions:
1. With extra olive oil, brush the tuna fillets and sprinkle with salt and pepper. Grill (or sauté if you don't have a grill pan) the fillets over medium-high heat for 3 minutes per side.
2. Meanwhile, combine the olives, red bell peppers, capers, basil and olive oil in a small mixing bowl. Set aside.
3. Remove the tuna fillets from the heat and pour the tapenade mixture over each fillet. Finish with a squeeze of lemon and a little lemon zest.

Simple Shrimp Salad

Servings: 4
Prep Time: 5 minutes
Cook Time: 10 minutes

Ingredients:
3 hard-boiled eggs, peeled and chopped
2 cups cooked salad shrimp, shells and tails removed
½ red onion, diced
4 stalks celery, diced
½ cup ground Dijon mustard
2 tablespoons white wine vinegar
1 tablespoon olive oil
1 tablespoon fresh parsley
1 tablespoon fresh thyme
1 tablespoon fresh basil
4 cups mixed greens

Directions:
1. Add the mixed greens, cooked shrimp, chopped eggs, red onion, and celery to a large bowl.
2. In a smaller bowl mix together the ground Dijon mustard, white wine vinegar, olive oil and the herbs. Pour the mixture over the mixed greens and serve.

Pepper Crusted Halibut

Servings: 4
Prep Time: 2 minutes
Cook Time: 8 minutes

Ingredients:
1 tablespoon black pepper
1 tablespoon fresh lemon juice
1 teaspoon olive oil
1 teaspoon salt
4 Halibut fillets

Directions:
1. Heat up a non-stick pan to medium-high heat.
2. Combine the black pepper, lemon juice and olive oil then rub the mixture over each of the halibut fillets.
3. Place the fish in the hot pan and cook for 4 minutes on each side. (only turn once when the fish easily releases itself from the pan – otherwise you'll have a shredded mess on your hands)

Swordfish with Peach Salsa

Servings: 2
Prep Time: 5 minutes
Cook Time: 10 minutes

Ingredients:
2 swordfish fillets
1 tablespoon coconut oil
1 tablespoon apple cider vinegar
1 teaspoon honey
1 lemon, juiced
1 clove garlic, minced
½ teaspoon cayenne pepper
½ teaspoon black pepper
½ teaspoon salt
2 peaches, pits removed and diced
1 avocado, cored and diced
1 lime, juiced
½ cup cilantro, diced (you can substitute flat-leaf parsley if you like)

Directions:
1. Mix together the coconut oil, apple cider vinegar, honey, lemon juice, garlic, cayenne pepper, black pepper and salt. Lay the swordfish in this mixture and allow it to marinade for 2-3 minutes.
2. Next, heat a skillet over medium-high heat.
3. Place the swordfish in the non-stick skillet and cook for 3-5 minutes per side. Pour some of the marinade over the fish while it is cooking.
4. While your fish is cooking, mix together the peaches, avocado, lime juice and cilantro. To serve, plate, and top the fish with salsa.

Warp Speed Wraps and Paleo Sandwiches

Turkey Rolls

Servings: 4
Prep Time: 10 minutes
Cook Time: 0 minutes

Ingredients:
2 hard-boiled eggs, chopped
8 pieces thinly sliced turkey
1 cup spinach, chopped
½ cup red bell pepper, diced
½ cup yellow bell pepper
8 pickle slices
¼ cup shredded carrots

Directions:
1. Lay 2 pieces of turkey beside each other and overlap them on one side. Do this for the remaining six slices of turkey. (The turkey is acting as the wrap here.)
2. Lay the remaining ingredients on top of the turkey, then wrap roll the turkey slices into wraps.
3. Push toothpicks through the middle of each wrap to keep them together if necessary.

Lettuce Wraps

Servings: 4
Prep Time: 10 minutes
Cook Time: 0 minutes

Ingredients:
4 large pieces of lettuce
1 cup cooked shrimp, chopped
½ cup red bell pepper
½ cup green bell pepper
½ cup cucumber, chopped
½ cup tomatoes, diced

Directions:
1. Layer all of the ingredients onto one lettuce leaf, then roll the lettuce into simple wraps.
2. Serve with your favorite salad dressing for dipping.

Open-Faced Portobello Bacon Sandwiches

Servings: 4
Prep Time: 5 minutes
Cook Time: 10 minutes

Ingredients:
12 strips bacon
4 Portobello mushroom caps, stems and gills removed
1 tomato, sliced
2 teaspoons garlic powder
1 cup lettuce, shredded
Salt and Pepper

Directions:
1. Cut each strip of bacon in half widthwise and then cook over medium-high heat in a non-stick skillet.
2. Sprinkle salt, pepper and garlic powder over each Portobello mushroom then place them on a baking sheet and broil for 3-5 minutes. Pat out any excess water from the mushroom caps if necessary.
3. Once the bacon is finished cooking, place 6 half strips of bacon on to 1 Portobello mushroom cap, then add tomato slices and lettuce and enjoy!

Tomato Sliders

Servings: 4
Prep Time: 5 minutes
Cook Time: 10 minutes

Ingredients:
4 medium tomatoes
1 lb. ground beef
6-8 pickle slices
¼ cup shredded carrots
½ cucumber, sliced
½ cup spinach, chopped
Salt and pepper

Directions:
1. Cut the tomatoes in half and squeeze out any excess seeds.
2. Next, divide the ground beef into four equal portions and flatten them into burgers. Season the burgers with salt and pepper.
3. Cook the burgers for 3-4 minutes per side in a non-stick skillet over medium-high heat.
4. Once the burgers are finished cooking, layer the burgers with carrots, cucumbers, spinach, and pickles in between two halves of the tomatoes.

Red Bell Pepper Sandwiches

Servings: 4
Prep Time: 15 minutes
Cook Time: 0 minutes

Ingredients:
2 red bell peppers
8 slices thin turkey
1 tomato, sliced
1 avocado, sliced
½ cucumber, diced

Directions:
1. Cut the bell peppers along their grooves so that you get four flat pieces of pepper from one whole pepper. Remove all of the seeds from the peppers.
2. Layer turkey, avocado, tomato and cucumber on one piece of red bell pepper, then top with another red bell pepper.

Cucumber Subs

Servings: 4
Prep Time: 15 minutes
Cook Time: 0 minutes

Ingredients:
4 medium cucumbers, cut in half lengthwise
12 pieces sliced turkey or ham
½ tomato, diced
1 cup spinach, chopped
1 cup sweet peppers, any color, diced

Directions:
1. Cut each cucumber in half lengthwise, and scoop out the insides of one half.
2. Fill the scooped out cucumber with deli meat and veggies.
3. Top the scooped out cucumber with the other cucumber half.

Screamin' Fast Soups and Stews

South-East Asian Speedy Soup

Servings: 4
Prep Time: 5 minutes
Cook Time: 10 minutes

Ingredients:
1 tablespoon olive oil
3 cloves garlic, minced
1 tablespoon ginger, grated
2 Stalks lemongrass, peeled
6 cups chicken broth
1 lb. chicken breasts, diced
¼ cup cilantro
2 green onions, slices

Directions:
1. Heat the oil in a non-stick deep skillet over medium-high heat. Add the minced garlic, ginger and lemongrass and cook for 2-3 minutes.
2. Add the broth to the skillet and bring to a boil. Add the chicken and cook for 5 minutes.
3. Remove the soup from the heat and add the remaining ingredients, let cool for 2 minutes then serve.

Apple Butternut-Squash Soup

Servings: 4
Prep Time: 5 minutes
Cook Time: 10 minutes

Ingredients:
1 butternut squash, peeled, de-seeded and cubed
1 can coconut milk
2 cups apple juice
2 apples, peeled, cored and cubed
1 teaspoon cinnamon
1 teaspoon nutmeg

Directions:
1. Microwave the cubed butternut squash for 3-5 minutes, or until mushy.
2. Next, add all of the ingredients to a blender and blend until smooth.
3. Pour the blended soup into a saucepan and bring to a boil.
4. Reduce the soup's heat to low and simmer until time to serve.

Cauliflower *"Bisque"*

Servings: 4
Prep Time: 3-5 minutes
Cook Time: 10 minutes

Ingredients:
1 head cauliflower, chopped
4 tablespoons olive oil
1 teaspoon salt
1 white onion, diced
4 cups chicken stock

Directions:
1. Place the chopped cauliflower into a microwave safe bowl and microwave for 3-5 minutes, or until the cauliflower is mushy.
2. Transfer the cauliflower to a saucepan with 4 tablespoons of oil, diced onion, chicken stock and salt. Cook for 3-5 minutes.
3. Blend the soup with an immersion blender and simmer until ready to serve.

Mushroom Soup

Servings: 4
Prep Time: 2 minutes
Cook Time: 12-13 minutes

Ingredients:
2 cups button mushrooms, chopped
2 stalks celery, diced
1 white onion, diced
3 cloves garlic, minced
2 cups chicken stock
1 teaspoon dried rosemary
1 teaspoon dried thyme
2 teaspoons black pepper
2 tablespoons coconut flour

Directions:
1. Sauté, spices, garlic, onion mushrooms and celery in a saucepan over medium-high heat until onion is translucent (about 5 minutes).
2. Add the chicken stock
3. Bring the soup to a boil then reduce the heat to simmer.
4. Add the coconut flour to the soup to thicken it, and cook for 5-8 minutes before serving.

Creamy Tomato Soup

Servings: 4
Prep Time: 5 minutes
Cook Time: 10 minutes

Ingredients:
1T. coconut oil (or other cooking oil)
2 15 oz. cans diced tomatoes
1 cup coconut milk
1 cup onion, finely diced
1 cup beef broth
3 cloves garlic, minced
¼ cup fresh basil, chopped

Directions:
1. Sauté garlic and onion in oil in a saucepan until translucent.
2. Add beef broth
3. Blend the diced tomatoes and coconut milk together then transfer the mixture to the saucepan.
4. Heat the soup for 5-10 minutes, then garnish with fresh basil when ready to serve.

Hearty Chicken and Vegetable Soup

Servings: 4
Prep Time: 5 minutes
Cook Time: 10 minutes

Ingredients:
2 tablespoons coconut oil
1 white onion, diced
1 large carrot, peeled and sliced
1 stalk celery, diced
½ teaspoon dried thyme
3 cups rotisserie chicken, shredded
8 cups chicken broth
¼ cup fresh parsley
3 eggs, beaten
Salt and pepper to Taste

Directions:
1. Heat the coconut oil in a large saucepan over medium heat. Add the onion, carrot and celery and cook for 2-3 minutes. Stir in the thyme, the chicken and the broth and bring to a simmer.
2. Stir the soup so that it is moving in a gentle circle then pour in the beaten eggs. Continue to stir the soup and remove it from the heat.
3. Before serving, add the fresh parsley, salt and pepper.

Conclusion

Thank you again for purchasing this book!

I hope it was able to help you create some delicious, Paleo-friendly meals for your family in a pinch!

Remember nothing is set in stone to mix it up a bit add your own spices, mix and match meats or veggies and fully customize them to create entirely new and delicious meals.

Finally, if you enjoyed this book, please take the time to share your thoughts and post a review on Amazon. It'd be greatly appreciated!

Thank you and good luck!

Lucy Fast

Check out the other Yummy books in my Paleo Diet Solution Series!!

http://www.amazon.com/dp/B00HH1GBLC

http://www.amazon.com/dp/B00HH1GFRC

http://www.amazon.com/dp/B00HRMZE28

http://www.amazon.com/dp/B00HYKJCZ8